CITIES OF MIRRORS

CITIES OF MIRRORS

Hugh McFadden

Beaver Row Press

Cover photography by Joe Pilkington
Cover Layout by Shay McGonagle
Binding by William Anderson
Typesetting in Bodoni 10pt by Co-op Typesetting

Published and printed in 1984 by

Beaver Row Press
9 Beaver Row
Donnybrook, Dublin
Ireland

ISBN 0946308 08 X

Acknowledgements are made to the editors of the following magazines, in which some of these poems were published:

Aquarius, The Belfast Review, Broadsheet, The Cork Review, Cyphers, Oak, Poetry Ireland Newsletter, and *Poetry Ireland Review;*

and to the producer of the R.T.E. Radio One Programme, "Reared on Tales and Stories," for broadcasting several of the poems.

Table of Contents

*This collection
is dedicated to
Elizabeth Hayes*

REFLECTIONS ON TIME PIECES

Aye, there was a wheel too many
in this family's clock, too, Mr. K.
But then I looked in these mirrors
saw the reflections; you helped mend it.

NOT QUITE TOGETHER

Red-stone house
reaching into air
blue sky unclouded.
One gull hovers
sways
and floats down:
turning
it dives suddenly;
followed reluctantly
by another.

NOVEMBER

Dreaming of funerals
I awoke to birdsong
from the dying leaves
apple blossom long gone:
and I saw your head
framed in clear blue.
I will light a candle
for you. The year declines.
But see, here some flowers grow
and roses still bloom in
this seldom-tended garden

FOR JUSTIN O'MAHONY
Died 1979

Leaning against a Grafton Street wall
on a Summer's night you
played the tin whistle,
hair down round a face rapt
in its own music. People passed
some threw coins, young girls danced.
"Where are you going on holidays"
they asked, laughing, dancing.
"Vladivostok", you replied, playing:
"I wish I was in Carrickfergus"....

You crossed the dark river
soon after, left music in the air.

ART AND ARTIFICE

Nude, the flowers are displayed
in wanton abandon
opening their petals
to the five winds, while women
parade dead animals
wrapped round their haughty shoulders

DEMOLITION DUBLIN (1969)
(for Pearse Hutchinson)

Guard dogs beware....
do not trust the hand that feeds you,
for the men of great property
would starve you for a slim profit.

While the silent majority
money-plug their ears, you stand guard
in the rubble of old Dublin:
And the silence is deafening
to those poor enough to hear it.

But remember......
someday the voices of the men
of no property will be heard
again: and then, my canine friend,
it will be the long road for the old dog.

STILL—LIFE

Long empty halls are silent
pictures of scenes much too neat
and orderly line the footfall
deadened walls: a smiling girl
approaches me noiselessly.
Here people are kept like books
or samples in a laboratory.
Sudden awareness abruptly wakens:
old leaves tinkling outside my door
in the middle of a winter's night.

HOTEL IRELANDE,
RUE DU NORD.

Please leave on the light.
It gets very dark
and cold in here
when they turn the key.

ON THE DEATH OF KEATS

Confined in space you lay
dying, consumed by life.
From the steps of flowers
the aroma stifled your last breath.
Around your withering frame
a final mist came to your mind,
Enfield's cricket fields far behind.
And the drooping violet lay
on your brow, day-weary.

In an Italian room you died
in Ara Coeli, among Pan, Ceres
and Diana's friend, the hound.
You are not lost, as you knew,
but numbered among the saints:
Anglican, Catholic, Orthodox and Jew.
Now one with the immortal ashes
you are at rest at last.
Writ in water and in cloud......
Keats, sensitive, angelic and proud.

A BLACK CAT PURRED AND PADDED
AROUND SHELLEY'S GRAVE

After the noise of the city
it was a sweet release
to rest in the cemetery.
Flowers bloomed everywhere
peace suffused the air:
we left red petals there
and went to visit Keats.
Later we returned and
found a flower wilting
in the heat of the sun.
At Shelley's grave we stood
reading on stone his legend
"Nothing of him that doth fade"
while round that fragrant spot
a black cat purred and padded.

ELEGY FOR A CITY

O Rome of the small hills and large churches
crippled beggars lie in the shade
of Vaticano's fortress wall.
Now Mammon has it made
Lira and dollar are all.
Clerics pass by with briefcases
tourists finger the silk scarves.
In the Sistine chapel a babble
of Babel voices, heads back
electronic devices buzz in ears.
I thought of the sack of Rome
the barbarian, the passing years.
Once this was a chapel
prayerful, Michaelangelo blinded
by his own colours. And
I longed to blow a conch shell
Reawaken a lost spell. Once
Columbanus found here a home.
On the Basilica's steps in the dawn
I lay down, dreaming of heaven,
knocking on the door. O Santa
Maria Maggiore of the snow vision
here I found peace and rested:
Also in Trastevere, Santa Maria
and in the church of Santa Cecilia
cool in the crypt, music floated down
a golden voice wafted through stone
across the forgotten ages.

But it was in the hot afternoon
I shared joy with the one-legged man
and the Roman with Brando's face
in San Gallicano of the Roses.
The muse smiled through laughing eyes
then I found to my surprise
there was no need for a dictionary.
On the last night looking for love
we saw the piazza bathed in light
from a full moon. Around the fountain
music played, water splashed and
mothers ran after happy children.
We knew then it was possible
for a moment we might know it —
the elusive spirit which never dies
but sleeps in the hearts of all.

SUDDEN DEATH

Pompeii was the saddest place:
not the ruined temples
or their former splendour,
but the shells of houses
clustered together silently;
and the family of three
turned on their sides
caught in eternity.

JUST BEFORE THE DAWN

In the Dean's house at twenty
to four in the new morning
everything seems peaceful as
most of his guests sleep. Silence
envelops like a woman
in a loving embrace.
Outside in the garden
flowers, some folded, gently
glow in light from my window.
A white rose, a love sentry,
reminds me of you then
and stays with me until dawn.
The dew begins to form
on its silken petals.
I write on and think of you.

PARTING

Framed by massive steel gates
we stand closely together,
kissing, eyes closed tightly
feeling the soft roll of lips.
The traffic rumbles by and
then you cross over that line
leaving the space I live in.
Turning, you wave goodbye
your figure a frozen still
in my living memory:
highlighting, stressing the
moment of departure. Now
you show your back to me
the wind ruffling your brown curls.
I watch you go and wheel
retreating down the straight path
domed by embracing branches,
two lines of tall autumn beeches
lead forward to aloneness
and back to an instant
of bittersweet happiness.

HOT AND COLD

(for an erstwhile friend)

What earthquake, what fierce eruption
turned your flesh heart to pumice stone?
Does volcanic lava fill your viens
and fiery smoke pour from your brains?
No, but German Alps might suit you better:
a frozen lake, snowdrifts and a glacier.

SECOND BIRTHDAY OUTING

(For Hugh Christopher)

There was a fresh breeze that Summer
afternoon we went to the strand
at Sandymount. The tide was out
so far it merged with the horizon.
A boy, about nine, flew a red kite
in the skyblue flecked with white.
You walked along holding my hand 'till
I saw light running through a pool
abandoned by the tide. I took off
your new sandals so you could wade
in the water. Later, we found shells
embedded in the ridged beach and you
first discovered seaweed. Before we
left I traced James Joyce's name in
soft sand: then, as an afterthought,
added yours (and mine). You laughed
dancing happily on the letters.

ON HIS OWN TWO FEET

Niall at one deserves a poem.
Standing upright in a suit
buttercup yellow head to foot,
he's the king of his own room
without the slightest hint of gloom.
Face on camera, devoid of care,
curtain backdrop and high chair
he looks the lens straight in the eye
and doesn't fear what he will see.
Why should he? There's plenty time
to learn how sand full in the glass
filters away through the narrow pass.

AFTER THE ISLINGTON OF PATRICK KAVANAGH

(For John Jordan)

I play with my children
in Harold's Cross Green
I ascend to their own height
as tall as I've ever been.

TO THE GIRL WHO INSISTED YOU WERE
MARTIN COMERFORD

(I.M. Patrick Layde d. 9th Feb. '83.)

I would give you Ledwidge's youthful rose
but it has blown down that immortal
road from Slane to Drogheda. Therefore
it will have to be my own clematis
blossoming again at the garden wall
in September, twice in the same year.

O mystical sign of Spring returning
while the leaves tumble forever in
the yellowing Green of Harold's Cross
you'll remember the hour we spent together.

COLOUR

Yellow the pen as when a child
coloured with crayon a giant's walk
Through purple, black and forests blue
where flowers grew in unearthly hue,
Green were his feet and the huge stalk
where Jack in red and spirit mild
slew the monster in the eye of a child:
and they all came tumbling down.
Ring-a-ring-a-rosy, I'll tell you a story
If you're good and if you're glad
I'll put you gently up to bed.
But chasing round and round was better,
then what wonder at the weather.
Would Jack, the beanstalk, even the monster
survive the howling Winter shower?
And when will daddy chop the tree
where giants live in strange harmony?

FOR MY ELDER SON, HUGH, AND MY FATHER.

At three years old your adventure is
to fly in a plane into rocket space
above the green earth, beneath blue sky;
feeling a mixture of fear and joy
and wonder at this metal machine

which takes you well on your way to heaven:
while men sit talking, laughing, smoking
and, seat belts unfastened, get down to gulping.

At that same age my own thrill once was
Atlantic Rollers breaking, foaming,
and the mystery of water green, blue,
thundering in rhythm cosmically set.

My father promised a sixpenny bit
if I didn't cry but bravely ventured
into an enormous wave threat'ning
to sweep me clear off two sandy feet.
I called for his help, throwing out arms
to this smiling brown-haired handsome man
who laughed and gave me sanctuary
and also the wondrous silver penny.

If, someday, I'm as rich as Getty
I won't forget that magic money:
for the love he showed me for the sea
has proved a lifetime's treasure to me.

My hope is that your first plane journey
will stay as long in adult memory.

WHITE HEAT IN HERAKLION

On the way to visit the great mound tomb
of the saintly Kazantzakis at noon
white heat reflected from houses entwined
with purple, crimson and vivid blue flowers.
The old Cretan women said: "Go back.
It's siesta, Meltami, hot Sahara".
And I knew we risked a real sunstroke, but
taking the shade wherever door awnings
offered shelter and a moment's rest,
we stopped exhausted in a side street.
Wiping our brows, drinking feverishly from
the blessed Malia water carrier,
washing our faces and hands in ritual
it was then I saw the prostrate, mistral bird
almost asphyxiated on blazing ground:
mouth gaping, eyes closed, feathers congealed together.
I picked it up, careful as a city dweller
frightened in case I hurt its lifeless wings;
and opening the precious jug of water,
anointed it with holy cretan elixir:
first on the eyes, next the feathers and then
poured the cool liquid slowly round its beak.
In the shimmering haze the bird fluttered
looked at its usual, hereditary foe
and staggered weakly on the ground, so
I called a young Greek boy, island old,
and with the assurance of mighty Jove
he embraced it in his hand like gold,
carried it to the house where blue flowers grew
and turning quietly said: "My friend, thank you".

BAR OBSCENE

In the plastic bar the blather
level rises as closing-time
approaches. Behind the counter
the banker smiles and simpers
oranges and lemons tumbling
in his ice-cold eyes: Jackpot.
A good crowd tonight, quickly
responding to his canny gaze.

Take your pick — a wealthy lecher
patting his corpulance as he eyes
the scheming innocent with the thighs
or the boastful, fashionable
murderer, red dye in his hair.
And that man there in the corner
talking to the Holy Spirit: he's
quite harmless, but more than clever
because occasionally he observes
and notes the deadly hilarity
as money accepts the bloody penny
for the last drink, in case plenty
cannot obliterate his child's memory.

AMONG THE BIRDS OF DUBLIN SIX

Gul of the Long Arms pirouettes
letting them touch his dainty knees
O'Ryan hides behind the myths
while Gul begins to shoot the breeze.

"This music that I hear tonight
is very strange and unrefined;
it must be from a distant land
unfit for those being wined and dined".

Aloft the dome is purblind dark
and deep; choppy flows the Liffey.
Gul, showing a sensual smile, says
"I'll be back in just a jiffy".

The Arab person starts to dance
tries to weave an antique spell
Shannon goes into a trance
clearly sees the girl's a swell.

The host is talking to his wife
for whom he plays a sparkling harp;
now the music comes alive
Moloney's bones give Gul a start.

O, let us have some rousing
music, a gentle woman cries.
Soon the golden voice of Lennon
lights Shannon's imaginative eyes.

When the boys begin to gather
in the centre of the room,
Gul appears behind the window
waves his two limbs at the moon.

He sees what those in the backroom
are having, so lies down on the floor;
hostess brings in warm Rioja
the quiet boy calls out for more.

Shannon waltzes the dark lady
before reclining with a grin;
Gul re-enters sotto voce
soon complains he cannot win.

Then the Northern lights cascaded
smoke poured from the magic bird,
the host puffed on his Sumatra
put on deaf Beethoven's Third.

At this point, climact'ric moment,
as ecstasy reached a frenzy,
Duffy's donkeys were braying near
the Church of the Holy Rosary.

And brayed within the Ros'ry field
when Hamlet donned his Dublin mask;
well, do you know who was betrayed
or do you really have to ask?

MEANWHILE, ON THE STOCK EXCHANGE

While the pundits prepare for the third world war
as though we lived on the moon
I switch off the T.V. and write
of some things that still remain —
the inexplicable hospitality of a stranger
a child's skin as soft as the bloom
on a rose petal, when it starts to blush.

MORNING DREAM

I was dancing in the street
to a late Fifties beat
not a soul to be seen
Buddy Holly sang "Rave On".

My friends were in the cafe
making love with their eyes
smoking and drinking coffee
thinking, my, how time flies.

Then the dancing turned to marching
crowds sang "We shall Overcome",
but a bony hand was beating
on that bloodstained old drum.

Too soon the music was gone.
Now the chant was revolution:
rubber bullets, stones, barricades
and C.S. gas stung the eyes.

It seems so long ago.

I was dreaming of John Lennon
playing on his white piano ———

We were dancing in the street.

PARTY PIECE

Trying to enliven
a surburban party
I recited poetry
to a sullen young clown
from Dublin city one,
who had the effrontery
to talk about money
and some business fantasy.
"Who gave ya permission
to read poetry to me?"
said this mercenary loon.
"I'm rewriting the Constitution",
was my reply. "and Article One
extends the national territory
to encompass the realm of poetry".

FOR MY MOTHER

You might live to see
the daffodils, perhaps
even the tulips, but
you will probably die
before roses bloom.

Slowly you fade
in a hospital bed:
never again to walk
on lush grass, never
to stand by the waves
listening to them boom.

Sealed off from sound
in your final room,
as the days lengthen
your night will come.

Soon spring birds will sing
but you will not hear them.

Frost-bright the stars
as I write goodbye.
Your smile I'll remember:
And that sigh.

FOR MARGARET GILLESPIE
(died Derry, 22-4-1981)

Your wide forehead was marble cold
when I kissed it goodbye, your
face set in a waxen death-mask
by the scalpel hand of pain.
The Rosary was said, chanted;
and I was left with your beads.

As snowflakes swirled we carried
your coffin to Galliagh chapel.
No drums or flags, only the sound
of feet treading an icy road
to the cemetary in Creggan.

We huddled together in the cold
north-easterly wind, snow gusting
across the graves and headstones.
Then the last prayers wafted away
in a white pentacostal blizzard.

On the way home to your empty house
burnt-out cars and mounds of debris
lay piled at corners. You died in
the Waterside, as youths rioted;
the Bogside disturbed again. You're gone
from all troubles, from desolate streets
and the songs about lovely Derry.

We raised a glass to your memory
before I left the shattered city
crossed the bridge of the deep Foyle
and headed South before night fell:
the hills stark in the gathering dusk.

SIGHT REGAINED

As I took you out to walk
in the grey February air
you stopped me excitedly
to look at daffodil shoots
struggling to grow among weeds
in my neglected garden.

And you shocked me into seeing
once again the anti-death expanding
in my tangled earth. Your joy
was blind to the concrete street
turning it into a flower-bed
rainbow-coloured on a dark day.

NIGHT MESSENGER

Silver moth in the black
outside my window,
moondust on its wings,
flutters against the glass
seeking a light inside,
then falls back into darkness.

The window is a mirror:
open it and see dancing
in the sun-bright air
a multi-coloured butterfly.

WHITE IN BLACK

From my kitchen window
I see in the dark winter
sky a solitary star
cold-bright as a diamond.

I gaze more intently
and discover two others
shining very faintly
near it. Then I realise
they are aeons apart
lost lovers separated.
Snow covers my garden
the last roses are fading.

TORN LACE

Two snow-beaded spider's webs
shiver on the back of a window
the December wind whirling flakes
in a melancholy, ghostly dance.
These webs are funereal mantillas
tattered remnants of a spider's desire.

AN OLD HAUNT

Very slowly solitude slips round me
in St. Stephen's Green. I rest:
see pale salmon clouds blossom.
I'm back in the fields of Elysium.

Silence is a silver foil which allows
the lost voice to speak again.
I commune with the bright shade of Mangan
then leave while the light still glows.

MINSTREL BOY

(for Paul Durcan)

You showed me Westport in
the light of Asia Minor;
and I sent you a photograph
of the Anglican Cemetery in Rome.
I remember the roses in your hair
the evening John Jordan emigrated
to Newfoundland from the Bailey.
Tonight, on my 39th. birthday
to heaven, I think of you and
Patrick K: how it used to be
sitting together dancing in our heads.
I haven't stopped dancing yet:
to the great dismay of the consultants.

ELIZABETH

We shared the ecstasy
listened to Billie Holiday
survived the pain
and made a home
out of many a room.

We rode the trains
held hands in planes
rock and rolled
through Sixties London.

With you I first stood
on the Champs Elysees
sat in Dam Square
and took it easy:
saw the Parthenon
wandered in Rome
plucked flowers in the Forum
watched the sun go down.

We're still together
after calm and storm:
you gave me our children
I give you this poem.

JORGE LUIS BORGES
reading in Dublin 18-6-1982.

On the stage of the round room
of Plurabelle's Mansion House
you waited to read a poem
bird-patient, Christ's church mouse.

You had come a great distance
to love Anna Livia
with your task force of sense
despite Thatcher, the junta.

Only you could decypher
words that transcend war
could make the rich sighted see
how blind their generals are.

Please move the sound boom away
out of reach of that gun
allow the poet to say
he's a very simple man.

            "Born in twilight
            I leave in twilight."

Use your camera flashes
or the available light
his gift is in the verses
for those with real insight.

THE SULTAN'S FOUNTAIN OUTSIDE THE WALLS
OF TOPKAPI PALACE

(for Joseph Agneta)

Write about this beautiful Cesme
someday, Hugh: you said to me,
as we lingered in Byzantium.

See, the old colours are being restored.
Isn't it lovely, exquisite?
Look, under the four cornices
of the pavilion's delicate roof
songbirds gather in warm nooks
trilling out their hearts at dusk.

It's a poem in stone to water:
a symbol, it nourishes all things.
Those intricate, chiselled and sculpted
patterns are fluted flowers, plump fruits.

Nowhere will you find anything more
delightful in Constantinople
than to watch the melting pot people
run their hands under pure water
reviving their bodies and their souls.

FURTHER ON UP THE ROAD

When you saw me drinking at the bar
you may have guessed that I had
a sweet tooth, but you were wrong
if you thought I was made of sugar.

TO ALL HIGH WIRE ARTISTS

Even the most agile
gifted performer
can walk only one
tightrope at a time
without a safety net.
And nets can be black holes
held together with cell tissue.

HOW AM I DOING?

Well
I'm hanging on
to the inside rim
of a fine circle.

So far, so good.

The deadly, hooded archer
hasn't found the target
yet.

How are you doin', yourself?

INNER VOYAGE HOME

In darkness
I lie and
view clearly
my body
disintegrating:
my own soul
becoming
a minute
particle
of starlight.

Hugh McFadden was born in Derry. He spent his early childhood there and in Co. Donegal, before moving in 1949 to live in Dublin. He was educated at Synge Street and University College, Dublin.

During the mid-Sixties he lived in London and worked in a variety of occupations, before returning to Dublin to take a B.A. degree in history and politics and an M.A. degree in modern Irish history at U.C.D. He was a college tutor there for five years, during which time he worked as a researcher with the Irish Manuscripts Commission and as an editorial assistant on the Correspondence of Daniel O'Connell (8 vols., Irish University Press).

His poems have been published widely in Irish literary magazines and in British journals. They have been broadcast also on RTE Radio. He has been described by the Editor of the London magazine *Aquarius* as "one of the best of the younger Irish poets".

Since 1973 he has been a staff journalist with *The Irish Press.*

He is married with three children.